The Same Ol' Me

Amusing Poems

By

Doreen H Reed

Contents

Copyright

My Cd 'The same Ol' Me' was recorded in 2012. This book contains the sixteen amusing poems that are recorded on that Cd.
The same Ol' Me© Copyright2012 belongs to the author Doreen Reed.

If you should wish to share any of these poems and tales, I do please ask, that each one be accredited with my name and website. **www.doreenreedpoet.com**

Doreen Reed

Dedication

My thanks to all the people who have laughed at my tales and encouraged me to keep writing and performing.

My thanks too, to Julie Fox-Allen of www.foxportraits.co.uk for the artwork on the cover.

About the Author

Doreen has been gaining recognition as a writer of observational poetry which is witty, funny, with a down to earth style which anyone who remembers the fifties or sixties can easily relate to. She is very much in demand as a popular guest speaker at functions, group meetings and special events around Lincolnshire and East Anglia. With a talent for originality coupled with a very natural sense of humour, Doreen's work is a delightful programme of memories, amusing predicaments and family observations.

The Picnic

Whilst caring for grandchildren
as grandparents often do,
they thought, to keep them entertained,
they would take them to the zoo.

They thought they'd take a picnic
to save the cost and queues.
What would the children like to eat?
Well, best to let them choose.

'So c'mon children', Grandma said,
'what goodies shall we take?'
They asked for crisps and biscuits
and Grandma's nice fruit cake.

They also asked for Cheese Strings,
meaning strings of processed cheese.
Well Grandpa overheard this
and he was far from pleased.

He didn't watch the TV ads,
he thought they'd said 'G' strings
and asked his young granddaughter
how she knew about such things.

The thought of edible G strings
came to Grandad as a shock
and he was most surprised
to find, that Gran had some in stock.

When Gran showed him the packet
he realised his mistake
and said they didn't appeal to him,
he preferred a piece of cake.

So questions from grandchildren
he tried hard to avoid,
when they asked him what a 'G' string was
and why was he annoyed.

But the young girl was persistent,
'please tell me what a G String is,
then I can tell my classmates,
they will think you are a Wiz.'

Gran tried to change the subject,
she was feeling really tense
but the girl said, 'c'mon Granddad,
don't keep me in suspense.'

Grandad then tried to hum that air
by Johann Sebastian Bach
and was relieved to hear the young girl say,
'oh I wish I hadn't asked.'

Grandma praised him later
for thinking on his feet,
he sighed and did agree with her
his reply was rather neat.

He vowed when children speak to him
at any later date,
if he isn't sure of what they say
he'll wait for Grandma to translate.

The Mirror

I was invited to go out with the camera club,
well the members were all very keen
to take an exclusive photo
of a special object, or a picturesque scene.

We went into a pub for refreshment,
laden with tripods and all,
I heard a 'Wow' from Kevin,
he'd espied a splendid mirror on a wall.

The pattern on the mirror was stunning,
to take a photo Kevin thought would be good
but he didn't want his reflection in the picture,
well, he tried every angle he could.

He climbed on a ladder; he crouched on the floor,
stood to the left and the right side too.
Customers looked on with interest,
one asked what he was trying to do.

'I want a photo of the mirror', he said
'but I don't want my reflection in it.'
Folk made some suggestions
but none of them worked,
I said, 'hey just a minute,

the solution is really quite simple',
members gathered to hear what I said,
I declared 'you move away from the mirror
and let me take the picture instead.'

Members uttered words like 'stupid',
and 'wanting to learn helpful hints'.
Well that was the end of my camera club days,
because they haven't invited me since.

Auntie Mabel's Genie

The word GENIE makes you think about Aladdin and his lamp doesn't it? Well, you may already know of course, that there is a type of bra called a GENIE.

My Auntie Mabel bought a Genie bra,
Uncle Walter he was delighted.
He thought if he rubbed it,
he'd be granted a wish,
I've not seen him quite so excited.

It was a bit like a liberty bodice,
with no rubber buttons to go flat.
The price was £39.95
and you got 3 bras in each pack.

They each had 2 pockets to house plastic cups,
if you felt you needed more support
but Auntie had a much better idea,
well, or so she thought.

'I don't need extra support' she said,
'my bosom doesn't sag.'
She'd put a hankie in each one
t'would save taking her handbag.

She wore it to a wedding; tears filled her eyes
as the bride and groom made their vows.
I cringed when I saw Auntie Mabel
fumbling with the front of her blouse.

The congregation stood in silence,
the vicar said, 'you may kiss the bride.'
Auntie Mabel was her undoing her buttons,
well, I felt I could have died.

With blouse all open
and searching into her bra,
to my horror she gave out a shout.
She declared, 'oh dear, I think I've lost one,
I definitely had two when I came out.'

The young vicar was clearly embarrassed
and so were some of the guests,
as Auntie Mabel stood in church,
fumbling around her breasts.

Old Harry Brown, who's 94,
said, 'what have you lost me duck?
Come over here and sit with me
and I will help you look.'

Uncle Walter, he was in the choir,
so he could not assist
but did give old Harry a glare
and showed him his clenched fist.

Old Harry didn't see him,
well his eyesight's very poor
but the kick his wife then gave him,
I guess that made him sore.

Like many modern weddings,
it was filmed and put on Youtube
but the picture that was viewed the most
was Auntie Mabel's boob.

She's been invited to another wedding,
on the invitation, would you believe?
It read, If you do come along
and we do hope you can,
please put your hankies up your sleeve.

Grandma's Budgies

My Granny had a budgie called Vincent,
she taught him to croon just like Bing.
Clearly a born entertainer,
for many hours each day he would sing.

'You must have been a beautiful baby'
and about being an old cowhand.
He sang of red sails in the sunset
and McNamara's band.

Grandma had a job at the White Lion,
she washed glasses & cleaned in the bar.
She took Vince there on Karaoke night
and soon he became a big star.

News spread like wild fire about Vincent
and how the budgie could croon.
The landlord he was delighted
as customers filled every room.

Takings were increasing daily.
The White Lion became a popular Pub.
Folk drank the real ale by the gallon
and spent more money on the pub grub.

Then the TV heard about Vincent
and wanted to film while he sang,
well this delighted the landlord
and of course, was a thrill for my Gran.

Gran polished the bar 'til it sparkled,
Vincent watched my dear Granny cleaning.
He had become quite a poser by now
and in front of his mirror he sat preening.

Dear Grandma was getting excited
while Vincent gave it some welly.
Gran wanted things to look the best
when her Vincent appeared on the telly.

She placed a big star above the cage door,
she did get a bit carried away.
His cage, she decided, must look its best,
it would be his dressing room on the big day.

She scrubbed perches and both his food pots.
She buffed up his looking glass.
Vince not only was a good singer
but she wanted to show he'd got class.

Gran decided to use the vacuum cleaner
to clean the birdcage floor,
Vince looked on with interest,
this hadn't been done before.

She put the cleaner hose in the cage
and bent down to plug it in.
Vincent thought it was a microphone,
he went up to it and started to sing.

He sang through the scales to warm up.
Gran said   'that was brilliant Vince.'
Not looking, Gran then switched it on
and no-one has seen him since!

Gran was quite upset

So I bought my Gran another,
she tried to teach him tricks
but the poor thing fell and broke a leg,
which Gran did her best to fix.

She tied a matchstick to his leg
to give him some support
but Billie, as she'd named him,
was clearly quite distraught.

He kept falling off his perch
and he was showing signs of rage,
as he tried to reach his dish of seed
in the corner of his cage.

Sadly, the match that Granny used,

had not been used before

and as poor Billie dragged his crutch,

across the gritted floor.

He found that unused matches

and grit do not agree

and alas poor little Billie

Is also history!

Mean Dean

Some time ago I went out with a
guy named Dean,
friends had warned he was mean,
they said,
'he'd walk miles to get something for free.'
I remembered their advice,
when he said, 'the weather's nice,
let me take you for a nice cup of tea.'

I prepared for the worst
and took my own purse,
in case he found a reason not to pay.
I said, 'you're very kind,
do you have somewhere in mind?'
He said, 'take my hand I will show you the way.'

We went into a hall; I saw two beds by a wall,
I said, 'this doesn't look like a cafe to me,
tell me, who are the owners?'
He said, 'no-one, it's Blood Donors,
but you will get a nice cup of tea.'

A Gift of Worcester

One guy who was quite fond of me,
wanted to buy a gift.
He'd thought of quite a few ideas,
in fact he'd made a list.

He knew that I liked cooking
would I like a cookery book?
I said that I had plenty
in fact they're everywhere I look.

He'd thought of clothes and jewelry
but didn't know my taste
and if I didn't like them,
then that would be a waste.

I didn't want him spending lots
'cos I really wasn't keen
but I didn't want to hurt him,
if I did, I would feel mean.

He wanted, he said, to buy a gift
as a token of affection.
Now I do like Royal Worcester
and have a small collection.

I said, 'I'd like some Worcester
to add to what I'd got,
but please', I said, 'just something small
that doesn't cost a lot.'

Next day he phoned and asked if he
could come and visit me,
so I thought I'd be polite
and invited him for tea.

I cleared a space upon the shelf,
to put it on display,
he'd know that I was pleased with it
if I displayed it right away.

It was wrapped up in gold paper.
I said, 'you've wrapped this well!'
He said he had asked an assistant
and she'd told him to go to,
a place in the High Street.

So he went and asked if they wrapped gifts
the lady said, 'of course.'
I bet 'til then she'd not gift wrapped
a bottle of Worcester Sauce.

The Same Ol' Me

A mirror never lies they say,
'though sometimes I wish mine did,
when I see my flabby cheeks and chin
and extra skin, on my eye lids.

I have considered surgery
but I'm really not that brave,
friends say I shouldn't worry,
I should accept it at my age.

In a way I am quite happy
with the flab 'neath my arm pits,
'cos I just tuck it in my bra
and it improves my bust a bit.

I was wondering about it,
when an old school friend called in,
we asked about each other's health,
then I poured my heart to him.

I made us both a cuppa,
he listened patiently.
He laughed and said, 'stay as you are'
and then said this to me.

'I had a good friend in my life,
she was known to all as Gabby,
her eyes were big and friendly
and her skin was very flabby.

She was happy and nice natured
a friend so very true.
We spent long hours together,
my friends all liked her too.

She was pleased when I was happy,
a rock when I felt sad,
she was always pleasant company,
the best friend I ever had.

She filled my life with pleasure,
I miss her so today.'
He said I was like Gabby
in a funny kind of way.

He then produced a photograph,
he still carries it around.
I could see affection in his eyes
for Gabby, his Bassett Hound!

Now I've been compared to some folk
but never to a pet.
Do I take it as a compliment?
Well I've not decided yet.

That guy is right in what he says,
so I hope my friends all see,
although my outside's changed a bit,
inside's *the Same ol' Me.*

A Diamond Wedding Anniversary Verse

My dear Auntie Mabel asked me to write a poem to put in the card she had bought for Uncle Walter on the occasion of their wedding anniversary, so I wrote this...........

We've been wed now for many years,
I know we've had our ups and downs
but on the whole life has been good,
we've worn more smiles than frowns.

I often think of our first date,
you drove a red sports car.
My old Mum said, 'you watch him dear,
don't let him go too far.'

My knees would go like jelly
when you nibbled at my ear.
I did feel so excited
to feel your body near.

You try to be romantic,
just like when we were young.
Believe me, I'm delighted.
you are still my special one.

You used to squeeze my hand so tight
and whisper in my ear
but many years have passed since then
and things have changed my dear.

I know you like to wink at girls
and give a cheeky pip on your hooter.
Sweetheart, it isn't quite the same,
now you're driving a mobility scooter.

Please don't feel hurt
when you're close to my ears
and I ask you not to bother,
'cos now you're wearing dentures
you've a tendency to slobber.

It plays havoc with my hearing aids
when the batteries get wet.
My knees won't go like jelly
since they've been replaced my pet.

And now for the romantic bit

As we've shared life together
we've had some lovely times
and even now we're old and grey
I'm so glad that you're mine.
So, on our anniversary,
I would just like to say,
sweetheart I love you even more
than I did on our wedding day.

T.A.

Three friends and I hired a holiday cottage,
it was remote, I can't remember the name.
We were thrilled to find an old fashioned bakery
not far down Honeysuckle Lane.

If there's one thing I adore,
it's home baked apple pie,
so I went inside to see.
Taking one from the pile
he said, 'this'll be apple.'
I said, 'they all look the same to me.'

He said, 'all our pies are coded'.
He showed me 'T.A.' on the crust.
'You see m'dear, that means 'tis apple
in Tom's coding I put my trust.'

To my delight the pie was superb,
I'd say the best I'd ever tasted.
My friends loved it too; we each had a piece,
I don't think one crumb was wasted.

On Friday when we left, I stopped and went in
and picked a pie that was coded 'T.A.'
'May I take this pie please?
We're on our way home,
I will have some for tea the next day.'

There's a guy who lives not far from me
who needs a good woman I feel,
so I decided to take the opportunity
to invite him around for a meal.

When he noticed the pie on the table
I could see he was very impressed,
I blushed when he asked
had I made it?
Well, I couldn't really say yes.

But I didn't say no either
and I felt that I'd not really lied,
as a cook I'm not a total disaster,
I could have made one myself if I'd tried.

I was pleased that my custard wasn't lumpy,

I'd added some rich Jersey cream.

He'd brought a wine

that was robust and fruity.

This date was going just like a dream.

With a heart filled with joy

I cut into the pie,

then stood there in disbelief,

it had 'T.A.' on the crust sure enough

but inside the pie, was minced beef.

His expression changed, I felt a fool.

He said, 'thank you and goodnight.'

It was too far to take it back of course,

so I decided I would write.

Within a few days I received a reply,

it was headed, 're-your complaint.'

On Mondays' pies the T stands for 'tis

but on Fridays' the T stands for 't'aint!.

Auntie Pat's New Dress

Auntie Pat said she'd like a new dress,
so I took her shopping one day.
I thought it was going to be easy
when she saw one she liked right away.

She said she would go to the fitting room
to try it, she wouldn't be long.
Well I was going to offer assistance
but I turned and there she was gone!

Minutes later there was such a commotion.
To my horror I saw Auntie Pat,
gripping a man with her left hand
and boy did she give him a smack.

The manager appeared Auntie shouted at him,
'there should be a bolt on that fitting room door.
This man came in while I was changing
I felt a jolt and I fell on the floor.'

She continued she always
watched 'Crime Watch.'
She'd seen men like him on TV.
Just for good measure she hit him again,
saying, 'no man is messing with me.'

I thought I'd best go to their rescue.
I apologised for this unfortunate rift.
I said, 'Auntie you should wear your specs,
that room you went in was the lift!'

Gran Would Like a Peach

Gran said, to her young grandson,
'I'd like a peach for tea,
they'll have some at the village shop,
would you pop down and see?'

She said, 'before you buy one,
pinch it, to check it's ripe,
if it's not sweet and soft you see
I could end up with gripe.'

Well, he came back with ten or more
saying, 'look Gran what I've got,
you see no-one was looking,
so I pinched the bloomin' lot.'

George the Heron

I thought I'd like a garden pond,
It's relaxing people say,
to sit and watch the fishes swim
on a nice fine summer day.

So near my kitchen one was built,
I could watch whilst washing dishes.
I went and spent a fair few pounds
on stocking it with fishes.

I looked out of my window
after breakfast the next day,
to my horror, a heron, thought my pond
was a nice fish takeaway.

I went outside and off he flew
but when I was back inside
he came and took another fish,
truth to tell I could have cried.

I returned to the Aquatic shop
and asked for their advice.
I was showed a plastic heron,
quite life-like and life-size.

He said 'this will solve the problem'
and then went on to say.
'heron's like to dine alone,
this will keep him away.'

I bought a few more fishes,
convinced I'd stopped his little game.
I called my heron Jenny,
well she'd got to have a name.

Herons may like to dine alone
but not so in springtime.
The heron was soon back again
other thoughts were on his mind.

Jenny stood still and graceful
and looking quite ornate.
The heron thought his luck was in,
he thought he'd found a mate.

I looked on in amazement
as he was doing his courting dance,
well, Jenny being plastic,
he just didn't stand a chance.

I watched him from my window
as I washed my breakfast dishes,
there he was cavorting
and making clear his wishes.

He must have had poor eyesight
his attention didn't waver.
Should I put him in my car
and take him to 'Specsavers'?

Well, this went on for quite some time,
I decided my next ploy,
was to take Jenny back again
and exchange her for a boy.

Next morning at the bus stop
stood Jenny and sad me.
I thought I'd use my bus pass
and travel there for free.

'Could I exchange this one?' I asked,
'for another one that's male?'
He looked at me peculiar
and turned a shade of pale.

He said, 'It isn't real you know,
I thought you realised that.'
I guess he thought me simple
as he gave my hand a pat.

I'd called the real one George by now
to differentiate,
between the live and plastic one,
when the story I relate.

I said, 'yes I do know that
but you should see the heron's antics.
He clearly fancies Jenny,
he sometimes gets quite frantic.'

The salesman looked quite worried
as round the shop I pranced,
waving hands and bowing,
demonstrating, the mating dance.

I attracted quite an audience
of ten or may be more.
He gave me a sample of fish food
and guided me to the door.

But then the man gave me a smile,
'you could buy another one.
He won't like competition
that would spoil his fun.'

So with a plastic heron 'neath each arm
I came out of the shop,
wishing I had come by car
I stood at the bus stop.

It was the same bus driver
and in his cheerful, cheeky tone,
said, 'are you going to breed them?'
I said, 'no, I am going home.'

Would you believe next morning
a few minutes after 8,
George stood there as large as life
and he'd brought along a mate.

The two of them cavorting
demonstrating the art of mating.
My garden pond appeared to be
a place for heron speed dating.

A pond is not relaxing
I'm just never going to win.
I took the plastic birds to a car boot sale
and had my fishpond all filled in.

My desire to watch fishes swimming
I didn't lose the will,
I now have two goldfishes
in a bowl on my window sill.

Flo and Daisy

A friend of mine asked me to write a poem about her favourite counties, Devon and Dorset, so I wrote these:

Flo gave the Vicar a smile
as she staggered down the aisle,
she was wearing little more than a corset.
He said, 'you'll not get to Heaven
doing that here in Devon.'
So she packed her bags
and moved to Dorset.

~~~~

Daisy, a dancer from Dorset,
was really too fat for her corset,
as she laced her stomach in,
the fat moved up to her chin.
If something doesn't fit, don't force it!

A Heavenly Kitten

Josie, an old school friend of mine,
called one summer's day,
she'd taken in a kitten,
it appeared to be a stray.

She couldn't really keep it
as she had pets of her own.
Did I know of anyone
who'd give Tiddles a home?

She telephoned again next day
requesting help from me.
Her dog had chased the kitten
and it was stuck up in a tree.

So I drove round to help her,
poor Josie was distressed.
We tried for hours to get him down,
we really did our best.

We offered it some cat food,
we called and tapped the dish,
Josie even went and cooked
a nice fresh piece of fish.

We thought he would get hungry
or maybe even tire,
I tried to reach with a butterfly net
but he climbed up even higher.

Although the tree is fairly tall
it's not strong enough to climb.
Then I had a brainwave,
well, I do, from time to time.

If I drove my car closer
and Josie got some rope,
perhaps we'd get the branch to bend
it was our only hope.

One end tied to the bumper
the other to the tree,
I drove gently forward,
we'd soon have Tiddles free.

Well the tree was bending nicely,
t'was all going to plan.
Josie called, 'I can reach him.'
She was holding out both hands.

Sadly, the rope was not too strong
and at that point it snapped
and like a great big catapult,
it kind of launched the cat!

I guess he wasn't too impressed
as he travelled through the air.
We didn't know where he had gone,
'though we searched everywhere.

We looked in neighbour's gardens,
in sheds and goldfish pools.
We didn't tell what we had done,
folk might think that was cruel.

We didn't check with Lucy
who lives across the way,
she wasn't an animal lover
and wouldn't let it stay.

We returned home disappointed
at twenty past eleven,
I hoped, by then, that Tiddles
had arrived in kittens' Heaven.

Josie called again next day
she had good news to tell,
Tiddles had found himself a home
and he was safe and well.

Lucy's daughter Susie,
did so want a pet,
Lucy wanted her to wait
so hadn't bought one yet.

But she said, 'a strange thing happened
only yesterday,
this cat had come to Susie',
she then went on to say.

'Today is Susie's birthday
and in her prayers she'd said,
she'd really love a kitten
and this one fell into a flower bed.'

They had looked on in amazement,
hardly believing their eyes.
Susie's prayer had been answered,
a special bundle, just fell, from the skies.

Josie said that Lucy,
was clearly rather smitten
and proud that they'd been chosen
to receive this 'Heavenly kitten.'

Of course we wouldn't tell them
from whence Tiddles had come.
We were pleased he'd found himself a home
with Susie & her Mum.

A Worm's Appeal

Not many people know this, but I am a proud owner of a well-established compost bin. What an exciting life I lead!

When I lift the lid I see an army of worms all working away and transforming my kitchen waste into lovely compost. Sometime ago I lifted the lid and dropped in the outside bits of a cauliflower and as it all landed with a thud on top of all the other stuff in there, I stood back thinking, 'am I hurting any worms?' Well they are only very small aren't they? It would be easy to break their legs wouldn't it?

So I sat and penned this poem on behalf of the millions of worms that are beavering away in our compost bins for gardeners everywhere.

For all of my life I've lived in this bin,
safe from birds
that arrive early or late.
You keep us well fed
and it's always good stuff
but I'm sad 'cos I've just lost my mate.

I see the smile on your face
as you peer in the top
and see us all working like ants.
You know that we're recycling
all your kitchen waste,
producing compost
to put on your plants.

When you lift the lid and bury us each time
with egg shells, cabbage leaves
and spud peelings,
I wonder, if by chance,
has it ever crossed your mind,
that even a worm can have feelings?

Last week a whole potato
landed on me,
since then my love life has been grim.
The worm that I love
is a distance away,
she prefers the other side of the bin.

I can't wriggle as fast as I used to
and you keep building me
mountains to climb,
when I reach her I feel so exhausted,
she says I'm just wasting my time.

Quite often you look in
and give a good stir
and I'm back once again at this end.
Do you do this for fun?
'cos I'd like you to know,
that it's driving me right round the bend.

Yesterday I decided to cling to the lid,
so when you opened it
I fell by her side
but the body felt stiff
and didn't respond,
it appeared that my loved one had died.

I caressed her stiff body
and said how I cared,
she was the loveliest worm
I'd ever known.
For me there'd be no other
of that I was sure,
so I'll spend the rest of my life all alone.

My poor heart was breaking,
then I heard her voice, saying,
'what are you doing with that stick?'
She's left me now for an intelligent worm,
she tells me that I'm stupid and thick.

So Mr. Gardener,

may I make a request

for all my friends that live in this bin?

We enjoy the good food

that you give us

but could you be more careful

how you drop it in?

~

I wrote that poem in 2003 and have since read
it to hundreds of people; I've read it on radio,
in theatres, halls, hotels etc. During the last
couple of years or so it has surprised me how
many people have come up to me and said that
since they heard it, they now cut things up
small and gently put them in the bin, so I think
there must be some grateful worms in compost
bins.

My Gran Loves Watching Monty

I'd heard, that, at the Village Hall,
for worthwhile charity funds,
there'd be a 'Ladies Evening'
of intrigue and good fun.

Well I am quite hard of hearing,
so I didn't catch each word
but the name of Monty, food and fun
were some of them I heard.

That day was Grandma's birthday,
I thought it would be a treat
and she does love watching 'Gardener's World'
so I booked us front row seats.

When we arrived that evening
the room was packed from wall to wall,
with teenage girls, young women,
no 'gardening types' at all.

Well, when I read the programme,
I knew I'd got it wrong.
I read the words 'Full Monty'
It wasn't Monty Don.

I turned to my dear Granny
and said, 'it isn't Monty Don.'
She said, 'I know, thank goodness,
this will be much more fun.'

I said I thought we ought to leave.
Gran said, 'don't make a fuss'
but if I didn't want to stay,
she'd go home on the bus.

The music played, the man appeared,
the young girls were soon screaming.
Slowly he took of shirt and tie,
my Gran just sat there, beaming!

Her glasses on, she watched wide-eyed,
she wasn't even blinking.
She chewed her lip and rubbed her hands,
Heaven knows what she was thinking.

Gran watched the young man's every move
as he stripped down to his thong.
Then he picked up a microphone
and said he'd sing a song.

He asked, any lady's birthday?'
Gran said, 'yes, me duck it's mine!'
And soon she was up on the stage,
their bodies were entwined.

When Granny lifted up her skirt
and showed her frilly drawers,
I did feel so embarrassed
but she did get some applause.

Dear Grandma was excited
I could see it in her face.
I feared, may be, her poor old heart
just might not stand the pace.

Concerned for my dear Grandma's health,
I climbed up on the stage.
I tried to get between them
but Gran's quite strong for her age.

I said, 'Gran, this excitement
could end your life you know.'
She replied, 'my dear, I do know that
But what a lovely way to go!'

Other books of Doreen's amusing poems available include

'No Socks to Wash'
'50 Grams'

All proceeds from sales of '50 Grams' will be donated to Breast Cancer Care

For details of Cds, Books, shows etc.
Or to book Doreen as a speaker/performer
visit her website
www.doreenreedpoet.com